The Last Song of the World

The Last Song of the World

POEMS

JOSEPH FASANO

AMERICAN POETS CONTINUUM SERIES NO. 211

BOA EDITIONS, LTD. ✳ ROCHESTER, NY ✳ 2024

For information about permission to reuse any material from this book, please contact The Permissions Company at www.permissionscompany.com or e-mail permdude@gmail.com.

Publications by BOA Editions, Ltd.—a not-for-profit corporation under section 501 (c) (3) of the United States Internal Revenue Code—are made possible with funds from a variety of sources, including public funds from the Literature Program of the National Endowment for the Arts; the New York State Council on the Arts, a state agency; and the County of Monroe, NY. Private funding sources include the Max and Marian Farash Charitable Foundation; the Mary S. Mulligan Charitable Trust; the Rochester Area Community Foundation; the Ames-Amzalak Memorial Trust in memory of Henry Ames, Semon Amzalak, and Dan Amzalak; the LGBT Fund of Greater Rochester; and contributions from many individuals nationwide. See Colophon on page 179 for special individual acknowledgments.

Cover Design: Sandy Knight
Cover Art: "Orpheus" attributed to Hugues Jean François Paul Duqueylard
Interior Design and Composition: Isabella Madeira
BOA Logo: Mirko

BOA Editions books are available electronically through BookShare, an online distributor offering Large-Print, Braille, Multimedia Audio Book, and Dyslexic formats, as well as through e-readers that feature text to speech capabilities.

Cataloging-in-Publication Data is available from the Library of Congress.

BOA Editions, Ltd.
250 North Goodman Street, Suite 306
Rochester, NY 14607
www.boaeditions.org
A. Poulin, Jr., Founder (1938-1996)

CONTENTS

III

IV

V

VI

Coda

SUDDEN HYMN IN WINTER

What if, after years
of trial,
a love should come
and lay a hand upon you
and say,
this late,
your life is not a crime

I

AFTER LOVE

Now that you have lost
the way you'd taken,
walk out through the new moon
in the spruces
and lie down in the deep leaves
of the clearing.
Listen: they are still here,
the wild things,
migrations moving on again from winter.
All your life
you heard a word
of the singing,
all your life
admitted just a bit of it;
all your life
you played your one
small part.

Wake now. Stay here
in your waking
and do it, finally
do it: open
to the whole of it, the whole of it,
the wind that sings
what's been since the beginning.
Listen. Listen. Listen.
There is no one
you're betraying
in your changes
when you become the whole wild song of what you are.

HYMN

Nec vitia nostra nec remedia pati possumus

—Livy

We are like strangers in the wild places. We watch
the deer swinging the intricate velvet from its antlers, never knowing
we are only as immense as what we shed in the dance.

The bride and bridegroom stand at the altar. Each thing
learned in mercy has a river in it. It holds the cargo
of a thousand crafts of fire that went down at evening.

We can neither endure our misfortunes nor face
the remedies needed to cure them. The fawns move
through the forest, and we move through the ruins of the dance.

Like Job, the mourner lays his head on the cold oak
of the table. His heart is a hundred calla lilies
under the muck of the river, opening before evening.

We think there is another shore. We stand with the new life
like a mooring rope over our shoulders, never guessing
that the staying is the freightage of the dance.

Orpheus turned to see his Eurydice gone. The Furies tore him
into pieces. *The sun*, he said, *I will worship the sun.*
But something in his ruin cried out for evening, evening, evening.

The wrens build at dusk. Friends, I love their moss-dressed
nests twisting in the pitch of the rafters, for they have taught me
that the ruins of the dance are the dance.

SHADOW PUPPETS

for my son

All my life I sought
a little comfort,
a little home
from which I once
was banished.

Now I lie beside you in the moonlight
and laugh with you
at the shadows on the ceiling:

these mythic things, these wings, these
bears,
their dance.

All my life my life was trying to make you—

you
who show me
this
is what a life is,

this living
it, this making
darkness beautiful,
this knowing that our world is in our hands.

PSALM

And now that we have told ourselves it's over,
we can walk back through the darkness of the garden

and look up through the briar to the first world.
This is the country of childhood, the new moon

like a filly in the willows, dragging the tatters of its saddle.
We have taken

the only road we had to; we have laid our hands
on the scriptures of our own hearts,

the pages frayed where someone tried to save them;
we have told ourselves

only mystery can live.
Listen, we told ourselves,

in the first days: if tonight
there is no one left to hold us, there is still

this dark and wild hymning; there is still
this new song

in this one world; there is still
the music of what is.

No more, no more waiting.
Cold

is the old, high way of changes,
and when no one, when not a soul

will hold you, tell yourself, when the wind comes
to hold you, tell yourself

that the end, too, has its splendor,
that the breath of it, the breath of it

is endless,
and whatever you have done with it, your one life,

there are the moments when the broken world is silent
and the moments when your song

is all you have left,
and the moment when you hold yourself

in our own arms
and the song you sing to the one you hold

in that coldness
sings very close to the song that would have been.

ENGLISH

What language is this
that equates *I love you*
with *I love turnips*?
Can we not have another word
for passion, steady passion,
the agony that launched a thousand ships?
And let it be fresh,
yet one we're used to:
I home you. You breathe me. We stallion.
If you cannot be a singer, be a story.
If you cannot be a story, be a song.
Say it, now,
to yourself, your love, your other:
I Rome you.
You Pompeii me.
I wouldn't Judas you.

WORDS FOUND IN THE RUBBLE AFTER THE LAST WAR

Yes, we lived in a time of darkness
and did nothing.

Yes, we looked up and we saw
the sky on fire,
and we knew that we had made the flames
with our own hands.

Yes, we wasted every breath
on rage.

Children, if any of you have survived this,
start again
with the simplest things, we beg you.

Walk out through the garden of the darkness
and touch each other's faces
in the morning air.

Slowly. Slowly. Say each other's names.

URGENT MESSAGE TO A FRIEND IN PAIN

I have to tell you
a little thing about living,
(I know, I know, but listen),
a little thing I've carried
in the dark:
Remember when you saw the stars of childhood,
when you knelt alone and thought
that they were there for you,
lamps that something held
to prove your beauty?
They are they are they are they
are they are.

IN THE CLEARING

I woke with the old fear
on my shoulder
like a lion's chin
smelling of honey.

How did it find me,
with my running?

I asked the leaves
what to do
with my agony
and they said

keep becoming
keep becoming

TO THOSE WHO TRY TO BAN BOOKS

I know
you won't be reading this anyway.
But maybe,
alone under the covers,
a child with a light
in the darkness
is opening
the first words of a story,
a story that your hands
would try to close now.
Whatever you do
for the darkness
that child with the light will survive you.

WHAT TO SAY TO THOSE WHO THINK YOU'RE A FOOL FOR CHOOSING POETRY

Tell them yes.
Tell them poetry is what chose you.
Tell them
you had a night, once,
just as they did,
when you knelt alone on the cold tiles
and asked the night
to give you a reason for being.
Tell them the answer was your life.
Tell them we are nothing, nothing
without passion,
the wild dark flock
that fills our rooms with joy.
Tell them
you will give the rest of your blazing days
to try to give another life
that moment,
that moment when you opened
to the coldness
and found that the music of your ruin
was too beautiful to ever be destroyed.

FOR A STUDENT WHO USED AI
TO WRITE A PAPER

Now I let it fall back
in the grasses.
I hear you. I know
this life is hard now.
I know your days are precious
on this earth.
But what are you trying
to be free of?
The living? The miraculous
task of it?
Love is for the ones who love the work.

WHEAT FIELD WITH CROWS

Try to remember the seasons
when the wind was new, when your hands
were good fire in the hands of travelers,

when the foliage brushed its music
against your body and nothing wasn't music,
when your future was the cool air in the garden

and to gather it was to know the losses
wholly, like songs composed for one hand
in the darkness.

Whatever you have opened to
at the end's door, try to remember the hours
when the sleeper walked unwoken in the night air,

when the wild winds rumbled past you in the fall fields
and you blessed them, you surrendered
to splendor, when you lifted up your ruins on the old road

and the hard law of the luminous moved through you.
Look at it. Look at the wind, now.
Stand there where you've asked your life to stand.

And if love
should come, its wool glove
on your shoulder, if love

should leave you kneeling on the roadway—
the bitter wind, the lost flocks
rocking by you—kneel there, in the dim

wind, as it sings you; kneel there,
as you must have done, in your first
world, when the wind

was wind, when your ruin
was a music—you
who were no one, once, and colder,

and were open so wholly to the brokenness
that you sang to whatever left you empty
like the cello in the cello maker's hands.

SAINT VITUS' DANCE

*"In 1518, hundreds of citizens of Strasbourg danced
uncontrollably and apparently unwillingly for days
on end; the mania lasted for about two months before
ending as mysteriously as it began...Such outbreaks
take place under circumstances of extreme stress...
[such as] famines...diseases...and overwhelming
stressors."*

—Encyclopedia Britannica

Given affliction, the body will find
a way; the body will turn itself

to music.
1518, and when the first of the dancers takes

to the streets, starving arms
akimbo, it is because

the crops have failed, the thresholds are plagued
with ashes; it is because, in the black mass

of the body's sacrament, the remedy is fiercer
than the curse—and when the searchers found

the neighbor girl deep in the forest
last winter, the blizzard lifting the worried fur

of their collars, she had stripped
naked, wholly, as the freezing

will do, the body gone mad in the last blaze
of being here, the body blossoming into music.

Once, the body says. Once
I knew a woman

whose madness took the shape of infinite music
filling her body

until nothing was left to her, and she became
water, fire, a palace where her ghosts could enter,

departing and hollowing her
at will. It was not grace,

exactly. And when
they left, for good, and left her

with nothing, she became
the same song that the world would have sung

without her. She stood
above the promise of some river

and looked back into the city
of her one life, its fallow fields

and endless choirs of fire,
and she heard, in time, the music,

and she became, in time, the music,
and she listened for how it asked itself

to end.
Think of it: the first step

forward, the tired soul like its own plague
in its blazing, lifting up its mild eyes

for the dancing.
Think of it: the rising up, the wonder.

Think of it: the brokenness,
the holding. And then the moment

when you look up at the wild skies,
your one life

in blazing flames around you—
the moment

when you do it, then, you do it:
the one thing the flesh can do

with ruin, the one thing
the doomed can do

in ruin,
the ruined ones, who rise

again, in fever,
and are briefly, briefly

like the saved ones,
whose maddened dance of splendor

is their rest.

THE MOON

I, too, am tired of it. And yet, like an old love,
it comes to us, illuminating the bare walls

of our houses, catching its hems
on our thresholds, carrying its little cup of blossoms.

We are done with it.
Aren't we done with it?

We have told ourselves
only grace can change us;

we have told ourselves
the craft is not the magic;

we have told ourselves
the myths are in our hands.

And yet, Issa wrote to us, *and ever.*
Let us walk out to the summer grass

and be there. Let us look up through the deepest leaves
and open. Let us wait, then,

while the ancient things
are woken, because haven't

we always been lonely,
haven't we looked up

into the wild skies
and asked, too, to be luminous

and ruined,
and risen like this cold stone in the darkness

and changed in it as radiantly as we can?

PIETÀ

for the mothers

All his life he'd wearied her with trials,
the hours he made her
chase him through the temple,
the times she let him
walk out through the wilderness,
the times he made her
lift his cross, his youth.
But all of it
has come to this, this stillness.
Waken, she wants to tell him,
waken.
And when she wipes his hair
from off his face
of changes,
when she leans down
to his scent of groves
and soldiers,
she whispers him,
in soft words
earth has earned her,
the one prayer
of a queen, a love,
a mother:
Let me once more carry it for you.

LETTER TO LORCA WRITTEN ON HIS PIANO, GRANADA, 2019

An ocean away, my country is dying.

Traveler,
I have had to touch
these dark keys
of your shadow

to know we feel our griefs
ahead of us
with their cargo

like great ships passing in the darkness
as we wade out, naked, through the shallows.

I have had to ask my own ghosts
where they go.

Come, you say,
come with me
awhile.

If the heart
is a dark horse on the roadway,
you can follow it

with its black tack
and its saddle,

follow it
in the mad hands of its captors,
dark bread loaded on its shoulders.

You can listen to the last good songs of earth.

Listen: it is late now.
It is later.

I have touched the maddened jasmine
in your garden;
I have smoothed the sheets
you rumpled when they took you;
I have lain down
in your linens
nothing burned.

Go, then. It is late.
The world is burning.

Córdoba,
Santaella,
Ángel—

And when they knelt you
in the new moon
on that lost road,

when your body
was a country that couldn't love you,

did you look up
at the dark stars in their gardens
and hear the night air, the silences, the wind's hands?

I had wanted, yes,
to leave this
in the wind's hands,

but I hear you, now,
I hear you
now, I do:

Go, now. Your life waits
on the roadway.
Walk it back
through the dark sleep of its captors.

Love someone like the last song of the world.

II

WORDS WHISPERED TO A
CHILD UNDER SIEGE

No, we are not going to die.
The sounds you hear
knocking the windows and chipping the paint
from the ceiling, that is a game
the world is playing.
Our task is to crouch in the dark as long as we can
and count the beats of our own hearts.
Good. Like that. Lay your hand
on my heart and I'll lay mine on yours.
Which one of us wins
is the one who loves the game the most
while it lasts.
Yes, it is going to last.
You can use your ear instead of your hand.
Here, on my heart.
Why is it beating faster? For you. That's all.
I always wanted you to be born
and so did the world.
No, those aren't a stranger's bootsteps in the house.
Yes, I'm here. We're safe.
Remember chess? Remember
hide-and-seek?
Remember the song your mother sang?
Let's sing that one.
She's still with us, yes. But you have to sing
without making a sound. She'd like that.
No, those aren't bootsteps.
Sing. Sing louder.
Those aren't bootsteps.
Let me show you how I cried when you were born.
Those aren't bootsteps.
Those aren't sirens.
Those aren't flames.

Close your eyes. Like chess. Like hide-and-seek.
When the game is done you get another life.

GAMES

(with each line ending with one of my son's first words)

Someday you will wake and read the books
I wrote when I was young and saying no
to joy, to love, and why I couldn't look
at what was good. And I will never know.

Ask me if the moon is not afraid.
I think it is, if something can be stone
and still alive, as I was all those days
I didn't think I'd find you in the cold.

But now you wake and find me at my chess—
trying light with darkness, learning how—
and climb to me, and give my king a throw,

and laugh at me, and look at me again
as though to ask what game we're playing now.
No games, Love. You win. I give. Hello.

THE LAST LOVE POEM

would have in it
a mother, a child
in a cellar,
hiding as the sky began its falling.

(Look what's left
of the place where they were hiding:
a diary, a scrap of bread, a toy.)

And then, very softly, as the bootsteps came,
a mother lifting water
to the child's lips

saying *your father*
was like soft rain in my orange trees.
Never forget you were made in wild joy.

NOSTOS

for my son

Can we talk about the moon?
About the way
it isn't done with us, not at all?
The way it comes into our houses
like a child with a boot full of sparrows
and sits at the foot of the bed
and says you will be changed.
It's true. You will.
I am trying to tell you you won't be ready.
I am trying to tell you joy
is a wild flock that only visits
our branches.
And yet
it stays;
they stay,
sometimes, those ghosts.

Love, this poem was going to be so long,
so full
of the stories that I wrote for you,
heroes and goblins and new
moons,
but I hear you now
calling from the other room
and I'm on my way to lie in quiet beside you
and lay my hand on the sparrow
of your little heart
that sings
and sings
and won't stay when it wakens.
Everyone is born so far from home.

CHILDHOOD

"...having to go on bewilders us"

—Rilke

When we have come to the end
of its thickets; when we have gone back,

one last time, to the houses;
when we have shut away

the old books of our hours,
we can step out, at last, through the thresholds,

the voices of the lost ones
in the doorways

like all of the foliage
of October; we can open

to the old ghosts in those deep
leaves; we can wade out

through the heft of them,
in wind.

Listen. There are night-birds
in the air tonight, the new moon

moving through the spruces
like a roan colt spitting its silver.

This
is the way, now, the only way.

This
is the middle of the singing.

And when you walk out
through the thick of it

and listen, when you kneel there
with the moon's mane

in your fingers,
let it come,

that thrashed
and tattered bridle;

take them, now,
the great reins

of your changes.
Who is it you would lose

if you forgave them
since the wild and the ruinous beginning?

WORDS TO SAY WHEN WALKING OUT THE DOOR

Yes, you will be damaged.

You will fail sometimes
and wildly.

Grief may snag its antlers
in your branches
before it leaves you,
before it finds its way.

Life, my one life,
can you hear me?
Someone in the sleep they call their waking
will crush your wonder,
and you will crush their wonder.

Bring your wonder; bring it anyway.

FOR THE PERSON WHO ASKED ME WHY
I POST MY POEMS ON SOCIAL MEDIA

Because there isn't time.
Because I want you to know
the things you say to yourself
in the darkness
are the right things.
Because you are the right thing.
You see the world? It is burning.
I want you to know words are burning.
Because to say one wrong word
is not a crime
but to live your life without maddening passion
is unforgivable, unforgivable.
Because I have only
a few sweet days
and my own mad heart—
its holy ghosts, its openings, its storms.
Because even if this
didn't save you,
didn't you read this believing
in the one hope it's shown you
you are holding:
that with the right words
you could still be transformed?

FOR A FRIEND MOURNING A TEACHER

I know
there is nothing I can say to you.
I know
how that life found you
in the shadows
and led you to the blackboard
in your borrowed clothes
and showed you that your own life
had the answers.
I know how someone
takes away the night.

Lay your little gift upon the empty desk.
I promise
we are made of those
who save us.
Every day
you'll face a greater question.

They live again each time you get it right.

FOR THE ONE WHO WILL HAVE MY BED
IN THE PSYCH WARD

So it happens the darkness did not take you.
So it happens you stand before the mirror
and shake away the grave-clothes
from your shoulders.
So it happens your shadow's wings
are furled.

Listen. Sit down
at the table
and break the bread, and drink
your little water,
and do not ask
why you deserve this mercy.

Someone, maybe you, must want this.
Stay here. Eat. You have to.
To save yourself is to save a stranger's world.

THE SINGING

Remember the days when your life
was always music?

Yes,
those days
are over.
That is gone.

But still there is the blazing
of the changes—
your heart like a mute swan in the fires.
Find someone
in this world of furious burning
who hears your life's great chaos as a song.

THE LATE ARRIVAL OF THE LIGHT

When you find yourself alone
without a winter coat,
when mourning holds you open
with its fierce grace,
when you find out that every life
is a ghost story,
you can wade out through the garden
of the darkness
and lie down and look up
at the wild stars,
the silent flames that cradled you
in childhood
and which, because their dying light
survives them, tell you that the distances
are infinite, that the ghosts that hold you
are hands that vanished long ago,
and that no one, no one close is on their way.
Only you can reach your life in time.

PENELOPE AND ODYSSEUS

Not the moment when he slays the suitors
in the palace, their wild cries thicker
than history. Not the moment
when he shows them all his great deeds,
the dark scars where they tied him
from the Sirens.
Not the moment someone touches him
in wonder
and feels Hector's death,
the flames of Troy, no land.

Not any of those moments. No.
Not those but the moment
he stands face to face with only her
and takes off the last of his armor
and she comes to him and touches his shoulder.
History is what happens
when we step out of the myths
and see the real mess standing before us.
Love is what happens after that.

TOUCHING THE ANCIENT FRAGMENT
OF HERMES

So this is what it feels like
to be found out.

Come, love, let us stand
before this mystery.
Even the ages
cannot tame him,
this boy who says
your one work is arrival;
your one work
is to reach your life
and wake it; your labor
is to know that you are here.

No more, no more waiting.
Touch him, touch
this dreamer.
What would your life be,
what freedom,
if for only
one moment
in your going
you could feel behind the fears
        the greatest fear?

JOAN OF ARC

Look at her, her eyes
like sudden thunder;
the armor
only flames
can take away.

What does she say
in her patience?

The age of stone
is over.
Turn
with all your fury
into the burning that will shake the world awake.

LINES WRITTEN IN A TIME OF PANDEMIC

And if the world isn't burning, it's burning.
    Fourteen days in quarantine, and
my love and I have danced, each night,
    in the living room—slowly, of course,

for the bones ache and the fevers
    come, the dry cough that scares us
half to madness. But we're well,
    we say—even the ghosts

inside us—and anyway
    the heart is impenetrable, isn't it,
clothed in gold like the Pope
    who knelt himself in a ring

of fire, in the days
    of faith, the better to be kept
from Heaven's judgment? The fleas
    went up in flames, and he

stayed down with the living.
    Living room, we say, and isn't that all
we ask for, these days, some space
    to tend our souls and keep our peace,

some space to lean back, by evening,
    with that forbidden cigarette,
to close our eyes as the brook
    beside us babbles poems and the lords

of money do their best to do death's will?
    Seven times we haven't watched *The Seventh
Seal*, Bergman's hymn to this
    world, not the other, not to see

the light inside the pilgrims' eyes
    when Death arrives, at last, to show them
what it is they've always almost been.
    I've so much left to say, is something

I would have said, when I was young,
    if I were knelt in chains
among that crowd, if I were face
    to face with what they see,

but it's evening here, the moon has come—
    and now I hear my good love's feet
climbing up to stand behind this door,
    her country voice of open grains and grace

that asks me if I'll open when I can—
    and I can, I am, I do, I open up
and take her in my arms
    and dance our stumbling way into the dark

and lie with her in fever on the floor
        and rise again, and listen to the dark,
the dark that has no reason
    not to rise, the dark that keeps

no secrets but the wind, the simple wind,
    which gives, and takes away,
and carries off the fragrance of our hair—
        and vaster things—the dead,

the lost, the gone, the flocks that turn above us
        for the spring, the geese
that cross above us in the night
    to find a world they trust will still be there.

ON THE WAY BACK FROM THE PSYCH WARD

I pull off the road
close to Goshen.
I remember the way
and I take it.
A mare comes
and lays her face
through the bitten fence.
What have we done with the immensity
that was entrusted to us?

DESIRE: AFTER SAPPHO

Like the lost gods astonished into being again
is he who sits where he can see you,
who hears you softening with laughter

and hardening with truth, all for him.
There lives in the human heart a music
like ghosts nesting in their one brief season

and it leaves me shaken, like a devastation
it shakes me. Let me only glance where you are,
and the wings are stilled, the music ends,

underneath my skin the flocks all lose their way,
migrations falter, the spring itself has lost
its way, my ears are shut with thunder.

And the salt breaks from me, the flocks
darken and break from me, I feel that I
have been changed, the dark birds

of death have come near me.

THE MIDDLE OF THE WAY

And now the same blank moon is on the yards.
A man looks out a window to the stars
and asks himself if anyone escapes
the blinding fires of childhood, the endless scars
of all the long-gone ghosts, their hands of flame.
A woman calls a child home at dusk,
forgetting that the name she calls is hers.
Thirty years ago she let it hush
its one wild song, that it might come inside.
This is how it is: no way to turn,
no promise in the dark. And yet, by god,
someone hears a calling in the night
and stumbles like a drunkard through the stars
and throws open the barn doors of the heart.

SONNET TO MY DEAD INTERRUPTED
BY A DOE IN FORSYTHIA

Time is what remains between us now.
How long must I dredge up each wild ghost
from out this coward heart like a run-out
bronco's bones that crumbled into snow?
It takes me days to assemble the wild things
that undo me. Love, hush, you have your gods
and I have mine. The dead have songs to sing
and they are rich and deep and sure and not
for us. Go on. Sing out. The years are years.
Eleven springs I've asked how loss is sung,
but the doe that eats my buds is back
at last, and I am done, just done, and
I want to start out through the marsh to touch
the shiver of it just because it is here.

ORPHEUS

How horrible to let your song awake
in a savage place where no one's life can hear.
I knew that it would happen from the day
I woke alone, when no one else was near

to soothe this brutal heart with gentle things.
So then I sang what's brutal in the world.
I sang it clear, as clear as fickle gifts
permitted me, and loved the humble work.

And then it came my time to praise the gods
of light, not darkness, all that makes us wise,
all that triumphs, all that can't be lost,

but still I'm half in love with what is wrong,
with all that ends, with all I can't make right—
and the moon that is the master of my song.

THE LIONS OF ORANGE COUNTY

for Lucie Brock-Broido

*In February of 1973 a local man purchased a pair
of mountain lions and released them into the woods
of Orange County. He had shaved the names of his
lost daughters into their fur.*

Cut it, you said. Cut.

If this
is the world, it is more precious

lessened. If this is the world, it is more.

Love, you said, and meant
a thousand doves loosed from the ruins
of the church of you.

Trouble, you said, and meant it.

Once, you said, once
there was another world. It came to you

like lions through the common things, lashing their tails

through America.

You said the heart
is the medieval basilica, flawless and unfinished

in a great plague.

You said winter, it was always almost winter.

(You had to. You had to remember.)

Tell it, then:

Once
you were the child
in the troubled well.

Once you were a relic
in your own hands,

intricate and buried there forever.

Look at them, the lions
in the tree-line, their blonde chins on each other's wintered

withers.

This is what we do: we live on.
We appear

like feral things in the fir trees, intricate and bewildered

by the script in us.

Tell us
what is written
in the flesh of us.

Rest, now, your lionhead
in clover.

Teach us what to do, sweet
master,
with the incredible afterlives we are.

AT WOLF LAKE

When we have put away the ghosts and the roses,
when we have closed the doors to the houses
of shadows,

when we have shut away
the voices of the lost in us
like dark harps in their locked

and perfect velvet,
we can carry ourselves,
like dark craft, in our own hands.

I know a place
of good winds and shadows,
and went there, once, and left it for you, in the open.

If you go, by morning, by the old road,
if you go there by the only way
you've left you,

I have left, for you, an old boat in the shallows.
Lie down and let the waters take you.
I know, I know, I know: the ghosts

when we're alone
are coldest music, but
if you listen, still, if you stay with it

and listen, if you make your way
past the snagged reeds
of the shallows, the new moon

like no one's hands beside you,
if you make your way
through all that wildest

silence, lie back
on the waters of that ancient place,
the morning tossed

like dark oars on the far shores, the spruces blue
in the cold light of the moon.
Listen, listen, listen.

And then, when you are ready, in that wreckage,
when you have told yourself that nothing
is ever ready,

do it, drifter:
look down
in those waters; touch the face

of the stranger
who has taken you, the one life
that has guided you

in silence,
the one life
that has tried, through all the trials,

when you knelt down
in the coldest snows, with no one,
to tell you you were only passing through.

III

TO A FRIEND IN RECOVERY

I know. I know
what hunger does to us:
the shadowy spoon, the glass
that holds the light.

I promise
they are not the light, those glowings.

Come home again.
Come break the bread
that trembles.

I will sit with you
through the hardest part
in darkness—

not always,
not forever,
not in rescue,
but until you taste the first taste of your life.

DOE

I found her
in the snows below the overpass,
the blue moon
in the broken bowls of her shoulders.

Time
will do its little crafts and magic

but always
I'll remember
how it happened,
how I knelt down
and held her in her wreckage
as she battled and ran mad in her fevered sleep.

My god there is no shelter from ourselves.

INVENTORY

This is what we have.
The hawk calling in the dark forest.
The hands of our lovers,
resting on our chests as we sleep.

And more.
The spring wind
waking us again
like all the bridles of childhood
dragged across our bodies,
still warm from the wild things that were broken in them.

The brokenness
is what we have.
That, too.

At the edge
of the road,
the doe curls in sawgrass
where the wreckage left her.

No one is alone on this wild earth.

Let sorrow come.
Let the rain fall
on the cold doe in the open
where she crumbles in the coming rush
of trouble.

Let the heart
do
what it must do, ruined

as the wintered lips of the broken
doe,

but opening,
sniffing the pistol.

TO A CHILD CRYING OVER A BREAKUP TEXT

Trust me, this is living, this
is living.

I promise
there is one word
that you carry,

a sentence that was given in the beginning.

Go in
through the wild doors of your own life—
the heavy thorns, the briars,
child,
the strife.

Lie down
on the far side of the forest.

Trust me, trust
me, trust me,

after all
the agonies,
to someone,

you'll say the one clear thing with all your life.

WATCHING A DOE GIVE BIRTH OUT OF SEASON AT THE TURNING OF THE YEAR

Every agony is a history saying *listen.*
When Timur had ridden
over the infants of Isfahan,

his battle stallion darkened
in its armor, he knew that we would turn from them
and live on;

he knew he'd live again
when we forget them, that the greatest plague is forsaking
what has been.

Listen
to the carnage in the dark tonight,
the voices singing *oblivion, oblivion.*

But still there is this wild thing
in a clearing
whose open eyes of cinnamon

and winter
tell us only the broken ones
must burn the world,

and the ancient things
await in us to waken,
and do you have any idea, any,

in your furies, how quietly the new life can begin?

FOR A BULLIED CHILD

They will say you are not
what beauty is.
They will say it
with ash in their own hearts,
all the ghosts
they refuse to know they carry.
They will mock you
as the darkness mocks the light.

Stay true. Their laughter means
they fear you.
You terrify them, terrify
with the *yes* of you.
And isn't that,
isn't that beauty?
Isn't that what beauty does, each time?

TRYING TO TRANSLATE YESENIN'S DEATH POEM

written in his own blood, December 28, 1925

And when he says *furrowed brow*
he means all the fields of Kostantinovo, open

and waiting for rain. And when he says *breast*
he means the little boat he slept in

where the Volga meets the Oka
and the wrens were gone. And when

he says *love* he means
dust, means years, means

seasons, means
how dare you take this hushed young blood

I hold out like a thing you cannot sing of
and say that it is not already song.

MIGRATIONS

And now that you have nothing left
but nothing,
walk out
through the rubble of your country
and look up
through the gnarled heart
of the garden,
the moon of youth
like burnt nests
in your branches,
the farthest stars
like antlers
in the snow.
Listen to them,
the dark flocks
in their drifting.
And that one thing
you must have known
in the beginning,
when you lay down
in the burning of your first world,
with your own hands
that had hurt you
into burning,
and you felt it, then,
that strange song
moving through you,
luminous and ruinous
and music,
and you knew
that it was no one's, wholly
no one's,
and you knew
that wherever it was going,
it would cast you out to where it had to go.

WORK

All day I've watched the wrens nest
in the willows.

Desire
sways a life
across its rivers
like a lost horse dragging its saddle.

And so? And so?
What will they say of me
at the end, then:
he was lost; he sang; he tried to praise.

The Egyptians, it is written,
faced their judges in the underworld
and told them everything, everything
they weren't.

Hush, now.
It is summer, lushest summer.
Another love
is gone again,
another. The wren stares
at her own nest
in astonishment, its little cup
of dust, of twigs, of hair.

And the heart, the brittle gift
we salvage?
The work you do
is secret, always secret.
You scrape away,
in darkened years
of secret,
every twisted thicket

that it isn't
and suddenly, if roughly,
    it is there.

THE VALLEY

So this is it, the garden
that you started from.
Something in you
knew where it was going,
your childhood like bridles
on your shoulders.
Something in you
made it through the night.

Wake now
and lay your hand
on the thrashing mare,
the foal inside her
waiting for the changes.
What have you been afraid of all your life?

TRIUMPH

That autumn my marriage broke
down, I got one. Don't tell me
it's a tired short story: someone leaves,

someone kneels there in the ruins,
wild to be wreckage forever.
In America you can buy

any ending, so I got one, all cold-chrome
and rum-red, 600 cc's of
adrenaline, roaring down the black ice of the Valley.

I could lie to you, forever, if I had to.
I could tell you
I found the country

within this country,
that I lay down in the feral fields
I'd come from, my Triumph on idle

in a spruce grove, and watched migrations
as they carried on toward winter,
and told no one, in the world's sweet secret

will. I could make for you
and make for you and make for you.
But why make a small story

anything: I was weeks
like that, tearing
down the Thruway, crashing

in the houses of brothers;
I was wilder and wilder
and wilder.

And when finally
I returned
to the old home, when I walked up

in my heavy boots at autumn's
end, my black boots
and my cropped hair and my death-

mask, when I slogged in and saw the strewn sheets
where she'd left them, I
did it, I lay down again

in the wreckage, I sank down
and then rose up
into morning, a rough

love, American
as anyone, rose up
and then walked out through the acreage

where the swift deer
crossed the dark yard
in their hunger, bolting

from my presence on that hill.
Mercy, mercy
on all swift things—on that cold chrome

where I left it
in an oak grove; on the night birds
where they passed me

in their fury, turning
in the world's sweet given will.
And on you, too, love, wherever

you have traveled—you
who've run the old high way
of winter, you

who've known the cold roads
and the bitter, you
who've danced the maddened dance

of splendor, in that rush
of love, where whatever is
is splendor—till

it stumbles, then
it isn't,
then is still.

THE VOW

When we are done with our ghosts,
they come to us one last time
in our new lives.

They stand on the threshold,
or in the kitchen
rinsing a bowl,

or smoothing a moon in the linens.
We are strangers to them now,
and they to us. We stand

looking past them into the yard,
where a child, the one
we never had,

runs through a sprinkler
singing hymns we swung from years ago.
Whatever we have done to them,

whatever they have done to us—
the words spoken in rage, the moment
we wept begging on our knees—

we walk to them now
and take them by the hands
and listen to the same wind

in the linens, the grasses
battering the transoms
like music we did not sing

to each other, the trouble
of the madness we once danced to,
the vastness

we did not dance in the moon.
It is summer;
let it be summer;

the rooms smell of jasmine,
of yarrow;
the cats are basking in the windows.

And when we've waited
in the late light
and its coldness, when we've brushed the dust

from off each other's shoulders,
we look up into the eyes
we had forgotten

and see there, for the first time
in ages, the lost face
of the one life

we have turned from,
our own face
in the mirrors of our houses, waiting

where it's waited
all these hours,
asking us, asking us

to come home now.
Say my name, it whispers to us. *Say it.*
And all these seasons

later, love,
we say it;
all these seasons

later, love, we do.

OVID AMONG THE BIRDS OF TOMIS

for Mark Strand

Think of him when he first understood
it meant forever. Think of him
letting the Emperor's letter fall

and stumbling off to stand among the birches
with his face in his hands, his long robes
blowing back toward the Tiber. Let it be

summer. Let rain sift through the limbs
and cover him with petals.
Let him be thinking

of anyone—a child, a father,
a woman whose hips swung like music
into the sea, her voice like a linnet cage

under water. He does not want to dream
of the mourner transformed into the fleeing deer,
Daphne sprouting roots to keep herself

where the gods can't find her.
He does not want to remember
the terrible lightning of transformation.

Let be, he is thinking. *Let me mourn.*
Look at him, kneeling
in the trade winds. He knows

what the wind is, and what it isn't.
And where the sails will never carry him
in their drifting. He knows

what the sea sings
as it burns.
Look, now: he is rising; he is silent.

And when he turns away
through the thickets, through the winters,
when he takes the way

through the sea's spray
and the lindens, listen
to the same wind

as he listens. He knows
what the waves say, what they've taken.
And what the singers in the rigging

aren't singing—the hush
of them, the dust
in them, this earth.

And that no one
may be with him still
to witness it: his triumph

as he wanders off
from his riches; his victory
as he listens, in the wintering,

to the lapwing, the saxifrage, the linnet's
wings; as they sing to him, in the clear tones
of the broken, the deep

and mysterious singing
not of long gone gods
or goddesses—not of magic, not

of lastingness, of after—
but the brief and sweetest hours
and the loss of them

the song was almost worth.

PENELOPE

They say you can save
your own life with what you make.

They say this, Telemachus.

Each night
I take the loom apart
in darkness, but not
because I need him

in these gardens—only
because I know now
what the doomed know:
we are only as sacred as what unmakes us.

Say his name
when you go to bed, Telemachus.
Then leave me, let me

say this to your father:

Child–you are
a child, aren't you–
I walk now
by these dark and hardened waters

and I pity you
the last days of your voyage.

For surely
you have long ago discovered it,

long ago
though the wind lives
to afflict you, long ago

though the dark
is every harbor, long ago

though you've broken
far from home.

Open. Be bold
and open.

There are the wild things
the Sirens sing
to take us

and the burning things
the Circes dream
to keep us

and the little hymn
the living live
with the living

where to go to what you are is not to go.

MARY MAGDALENE

In all my dreams he comes down
from that awful cross
and cradles my face
like the moon of youth.

I'm sorry, he whispers,
let's start again.
Ruin. Is. Not. What's. Beautiful.

CARIL ANNE FUGATE

b 1943: adolescent partner of accomplice Charles Starkweather.
Together they killed 10 during a six-day spree in Nebraska, 1958.
Starkweather was executed by electric chair. Fugate was sentenced
to life imprisonment and paroled in 1976.

Last night I dreamt of my father.
He watched you slip
a coin from his black silk vest
and replace it with the moon.
Then he kissed the rifle.

Always they get
the story wrong.
It had nothing to do
with James Dean.
We were alive, that's all.

I remember the way you held me
on the Interstate, the night
the pigs came.
Aint nothin right
in it, you whispered.

Then you kissed me
with those James Dean lips
until I didn't know
where the blood-black
clouds of America

stopped their blooming
and my youth began.
I know, I know.
But always my neighbor dances.
She pulls out photos

of her girlhood love,
how she slicked his hair
with Bristol Cream.
Then she can bury
those things with his shoes.

I guess I have to carry them.
Tonight I sit in my rented house,
and my gown is ruined.
My landlady tells me
of a boy they found

at the edge of the river—
half-boy, half-fish,
really—and lifted him
by the shoulders.
What does that mean?

I am old now.
You would not know me.
The young, divorced
woman I know
visits me mornings.

She stares at her hands.
She is still living
with the stray they took in
at the end together.
She is so beautifully sad.

But she has her life.
I think of the girl
trapped in the woods,
her ankle twisted
in a red-fox trap,

snow in her eyes.
I think of my mother,
the names carved in her blood
like a boat with no good
harbor. Nights, the dead

would come, once, sitting
on my linens in spring time.
How could I have done
the things I have
done, they'd whisper.

They meant themselves,
Charlie. They got it all wrong.
Now they are barely there.
Charlie, who is this strange dark
figure who stands by me

nights? She is clean,
and dark, and I do not know her.
Last night I helped two children
bury a barn owl
they'd discovered,

as you would the moon of youth.
Charlie, O Charlie,
what can I do?
When they strapped you
to the chair,

I looked away. You
who talked so smooth,
and gave me gooseflesh
when you found me
in the yard

of the Whittyer School.
That's all. Your mouth
was candy, and I went to you.
You who raised me
on fire

and spun me like a child
with their blood on your face,
the moon in your clothes.
You who laughed, and hid me.
You who will never have to live

through the worst part, ever:
Forgiveness. To be forgiven.

GENIE WILEY

"The house was completely dark; all the blinds were drawn and there were no toys, no clothes, nothing to indicate that a child of any age had lived there. The child's bedroom was at the back of the house with the window covered. The furnishings of the bedroom consisted of a cage with a chicken-wire lid and a toilet chair with some kind of homemade strapping device."

—Sgt. Frank Linley, after discovering the "feral" child known only as "Genie," who had spent the first 13 years of her life in almost total isolation.

They say I do not know the word
for love.

I do.

I know the little singing
of the blackbirds through the blackened

glass, the little wings
of my own heart
in darkness. I know

that what was done to me was not
me. I know

that something ending
makes no sound.

—Listen
to the furious birds
this morning.

They are powerless
not to sing out

to their hunters. They are troubled, troubled
into telling.

Tell it: You, too, were a music.
You waited

in your little heart of darkness
and you had a song

that not a soul
could know of.

I know, I know, I know now.

But how can I tell you
how to tell it?

Go down
into the wild heart
of the darkness.

Listen. Listen. Listen.

What silent
song, what wordless,

certain burning

will your one hushed life be singing

      when you're found?

PERSEPHONE

All my life
I heard a calling
from the shadows.
I knew
that one lost morning I would go to it.
I knew the moon
was lost foals from my first world,
turning
with their braided manes of fire.
I knew I'd heard
the things for which they fight.

No more, no more falling.
I woke
alone; I shattered; I
was no one.

Admit it, I whispered me,
admit it.

And then the dark god
came to me in radiance.
He came to me
and knelt before my kneeling
and held to me
the very fruit of ruin.
Why should I have turned from it,
my sisters?
Why should I not savor
what was made for me?
Taste the great mistake that makes your life.

SCHUMANN TO CLARA—BONN, 1856

Of my father I can only say
his life moved through him
like loons tilting toward a river

at dusk, not singing. He touched my face
the way a blind man touches bread,
as though he could teach me

where I was broken.
And he did. He almost did.
Sometimes I hear the wind

sifting the chaff in the fields, and I know
we were not made to be saved.
Sometimes I hear the colts

burning in the locked barn, and I know
we almost were. Fury
is not hard. What slays me

is the weight of it, all that unfinished praise.
I would like to wade
through the tired vines

awhile, lie down
in wild grape
and ivy, listen

until I heard no songs
in the night air, no songs
but the first hymns that could wake me.

Give me
this afternoon, this ruin,
the simple grace of each thing

in its shaking. Make me
the song I won't have made.
Grace

arrives to remind us
of the weight of it.
It does not come

to stay with us, to wake us. It comes
to lay its bridle
on our empty chests

and breathe its breath of golden bits
and linden
and stand again

and leave us, leave us
freshened, helpless
to tell the end from the changes.

POPPIES

Max Brod to Kafka–June 4, 1924

All week I've sought to write
just one word to name the flavor

of your breath the last time
you gave it to me. *Burn them,*

you whispered, lifting yourself
to one of my ears, then the other,

until you lay back
to watch the blackbirds gathering

in the dark pines, your tired eyes clarified
by hunger. No one knows

what I do for you, Franz. No one.
You told me the secret of beauty

is coldness. I know coldness,
Bruder. I know the odor

of the gold on the cold
hands of the dead

when they reach for you
one last time, as though you could know.

Poppies, that's what you smelled like,
Franz, that's all: the poppies Milena gave you.

Why should that word bring me
such comfort, the little weight of it

on my tongue, its scent of every ending
as I tell of it? I lie in your room now

and listen for the jackdaws
in the rafters. No one will know

how you laughed like them
at evening. No one will remember

the last oblivion you asked for.
Poppies. This is the century

of indifference, Franz, and I am a man
lying alone in the dark

thinking of poppies, thinking of you
thinking of fire, thinking of the wind

that sings our lives away
from one another, that carries us away

to be the dark. *Easy,*
you would have whispered,

say it colder, colder. I am done
with all this coldness, brother.

I am going out to kneel down
in the garden

and bury deep your last seeds
with your good gloves. I am going out

to where the broken loam
has turned.

The heart is not
leopards in the temples, drinking

all the holy vessels empty. A life
is not a chapel all in fire. We

are just the wine, awhile, brother,
lifted to the trembling lips

in darkness, stripped
of every meaning but the flavor.

Lift me in the hunger past all hungers.
Drink me like the last days of the world.

LOVE

Sometimes I still sleep with your boots on
in case I am you
in the dream-snows
and you're cold and you want to come home.

THE WRITER

Then Death sits you down at his table
and lays a page in front of you
and after all those years of
what you should have been doing
whispers to you, *save your life*.

AT WAVERLEY ABBEY

Say your life had crumbled
with its wonder.
Say
that you had opened
to the spring wind, all of you
resounding with its power.
Say the days
had changed you
into this.

Listen, now. Unbroken choirs
are silent.

Lie down
like these old stones in the darkness.

I promise you
your life is not in ruins.

And if it is,
if all of you is ruined,
listen
to the cold wind in the open.

The truest
and most beautiful part of you
is the ruins through which the mystery can sing.

WORDS FOR THE ROAD

Know, now, there is no one
who can guide you.
Know there will be nothing
to return to.
Know, now, that the trial
will be long.

Come, then. You were called to this,
this wild life.
Go in
and lie down in the darkness.
Hear them now, the wild flocks
in the starlight,
thrashing in the vastness of their passing?

If you cannot have a home, become a song.

NARCISSUS

Say you had stumbled,
all winter,
through the rough country
of yourself.
Say you had drawn the bow of your heart
at the dark edge of the forest
and let the does go by,
let them drink
from the dark face of the river.

It is winter, it has always
been winter,
and say you had followed them
where they were going—

through the willows, through the silence, through the dark pines—

and when you'd come, at last,
to the riverside,
you'd knelt down in the deep leaves
and seen him: a child
in the shivering
of the river,
staring up from the ruins
of the new moon.

Wouldn't that also be mercy:
to drag your hand
through that changed face
in the water

and to see, there,
at the scarred heart
of the darkness,

the moonlight that you must have been
before ruin

and the ruin of you
undoing you in the moonlight

and the brief and sweetest moments
when the two of you
are equally beautiful.

THE 52-HERTZ WHALE

They have called it
the loneliest of things, a voice
in the wilderness, singing
what nothing else will sing.
Is it
motherless, all that hunger?
Some last calf? The past
as it sounds?
Maybe. Maybe. Maybe.
But aren't we all
like that, roaming
the coldness of the oceans—
and you, too, half
in madness,
half of you that fathoms
you have to be your own song to be found.

THE WHALE SKELETON ON
LONG BRANCH BEACH

No one has woken with the gull-song.

You are still here. You are still alive
in this country.

These are things
you can do, still,
in the ruins:

waken;
unmake the bitter
linens;
walk out to the stripped ribs
where a heart had been

and climb in
and lie back
in its apses.

This shattering. These wildest
tides.
This earth.

Tell it. Tell it. Tell it:

Imagine being
so broken
and so lonely

that you thought you were
the wild song in a wild thing
calling like the dark heart of the darkness.

Or that you forgot you were.

POEM ENDING WITH AN INTERRUPTION BY MY TODDLER

All night I tried to find the beauty
in wanting. Now I wake
in the darkness
and scatter the crumbs of yesterday's bread
in the grasses,
the flocks of morning
flooding past my body.
If only we could want
so purely
that what we want becomes a song
water water water water water

WOLF TRAPPED

I found her on the far side of the mountain.
She had been there
for a week or more
and was tired. *Tired*
is a word like any other,
and she was past that,
she was past words in her agony.
She looked at me
and didn't rise
from her silence, her thin ribs
like a dark harp
in the breeze.
I went to help
and knew that she would hurt me.
I still have the dark scars to show it.
My lovers brush against them
in the lamplight.
They ask me
what the scars mean, what secret.
I sing *Promise. We. Won't. Touch. Until. You're. Free.*

THE LAND OF GOSHEN

Now my father wades out through his last sleep
and kneels down for the good touch
of his horses:

Cinnamon, Justice, Rum.

America has wrecked itself
with treachery,

but he waits,
he waits
for the waking,

and slowly, humbly, stumbling,
            Justice comes.

TEACHING MY SON TO SWIM

Maybe it was his blood in my veins
    that made me fight everything my father
tried to teach me. The right grip
    on the baseball bat; the words to say
to god; the way to wade, with reverence,
    slowly into someone else's life.
I could go on. Words. Deeds. The way to say

our name.
    Now, chest deep in the waters
of summer, I hold my little son's body
    across my forearms
and tell him listen, listen,
    he who does not know
I am only trying to give him a way

to leave me—this boy, this beautiful child
    with his nakedness, his honey-
colored eyes, this child I will hold like this
    for a few brief seasons in my arms
before I have to let go
    of all of it, all of it:

a home, a soul, a body;
    a father trying to show
how sweet it is to be held
    by anyone, anyone;
a son protesting, as they are made
    to do, for minutes, for hours, for years,
kicking and thrashing awhile

before he gets it.

THE KINGDOM OF WHAT IS

Now you wake alone
among the shadows
and lie back in the fires
of the moonlight.

When, you whisper, *when*
will I be rinsed of it:
this history, this bitterness,
this dust?

Let it, let the moon work;
let it show you:

There are moments
when your life becomes the darkness
and moments
when you rise up in your triumph

and moments
between one life
and another
when you lie alone
with no one there to know you
and to be the blazing changes is enough.

BOY LEADING A HORSE

–Picasso, 1907

Banishment is everyone's story—

and if you, too, had come a long way
through the desert;
if you, too, had come a long way

through the one rough country of your own life,
what would you bring with you
if not your own death,

dignified in its invisible bridle? What would you have
that hadn't carried you?

Say it: Once
you were a child in the wilderness. Once

you pressed your own face
to the wild thing, its dark heart

like a hymnal in the wind's
hands, and asked it, in clear tones, where it was going. Once

you kissed the blank script
of the lash.

Say it: If the world had broken you
like a bold colt, if the world had knelt you

deep into the soil of your own life,
would you not lay

your tame face in the red earth? Would you not say
what has no shadow has no way to love?

Love, we have come this far
through our own lives. We have carried

our hearts like tattered
saddles. Madness

is a music only one can hear. Madness
is the great mane

on your shoulder, turning you
toward a bare and troubled country, and no one

in the torn thorn
of that blankness.

Say it: Once
you lay, a great mare, in the wilderness. Men came

and sat there on their saddles,
watching you in the cold throes

of your labor,
old snow darkening their shoulders.

You have carried
the filly of your one life. You have carried it

through the mad heart
of this land.

Tell it. Tell it. Tell it:

The darkness speaks
to each of us in the beginning.
It holds our hearts
like a wild thing in its bridle:

I promise, it says,
you will not be given shelter.
I promise you
these three things
as you enter:

the deep green
and the mad hands of your breakers—

And the moments you're delivered
from your own ghosts
like a filly in the fillymaster's hands.

ODYSSEUS

He dreamt, each night, of the olive groves
through which she moved, the music of the loom
on which she took apart the life she'd known
and woke with it in ruins like the moon.

He woke, too. And always, when he did,
he called her name with such a horrid scream
that even hardened men whose lives were ships
of lost, dark bark would rock him back to sleep

as though they were the sea. But no words
soothed their hearts. For anyone who dreams
of home has heard the curse the doomed do:

Not Scylla, not Charybdis is the curse,
but you there passing quietly between,
the monster who could perfectly undo you.

TO A FRIEND WHO ALMOST CHOSE DEATH

You who almost hushed the song
you carry,
come to me, come
be clung to.
Let me carry
all of it, a moment.
Let me say your name
again, again.

Can you hear it? Can
you hear it?

Briefly, I can only be it
briefly,
but I will sing you; I will give you rest.

POETRY

All we have is a few sweet days
and naming.

White pine, blackthorn,
briar;
the new moon like a lost one's
empty bed.

Ghosts: we are riddled
with their singing.

We rise, despite
it all,
each morning—

the voices of the silenced ones inside us.

And isn't this, isn't this
living?
Isn't this what it means to raise the dead?

BURIAL

In one moment the earth
            holds you closer
      than I took a lifetime to.

ASH WEDNESDAY

for my son

What can be said that has not been said
about mercy,
about the burning world?

Tonight I rise from bed
at the sound of your cry

and brush away the moon's ash
from your forehead
that woke you with the soft weight
of its changes.

Hush, my child—
it is only the light
of the dying world. It is only
what the sun does
with its light.

Listen
now. Be still awhile
and listen.

Yes, son, we wake
into the changes—

And although the world
is burning, simply burning,

and although no word
can turn the earth
to mercy,

come, son, let me hold you;
let me hold you.

Let us say it with our lives, our lives, our lives.

JUDAS ON GOOD FRIDAY

And now we wake
and ask what we've forsaken.

Even the moon turns
its back to us, keeping
the secrets of its shadows.

Even the wind sings to unmake you.

Come, now. It is spring, still,
for the living.
Kneel down
by the vast glass
of the river

and touch the face
of the stranger
in those changes.

Tell it
what you said in the beginning:

*Come with me, come
with me, my one life–*

But that was ages
ago, ages—

Come with me, the one who can't betray you.

HOLY SATURDAY

Always we remember the agony,
a lost son kneeling in a garden.

Always we remember the ecstasy,
the breath of a traitor
when they came for him,
the mythic kiss that changed a world forever.

Always
we say to change is just to go.

But what if we have never heard
what we have to?
The story, we whisper,
tell the story.

But what if we were never story, ever?

Listen, the wrens sing, *listen:*
This
is the holy time,
this listening—

not the terrible Friday of the agony
or the wonderful Sunday
of the coming again

but the ordinary day of the waiting—
when they woke alone,
each of them, in the mystery,
or turned to face their lovers
in the humble light

and brushed the dust
from each other's
patient faces

and listened, awoke
and simply listened,
and waited for each other to know.

LINES FOR EASTER IN A TIME OF TROUBLES

Let this be the last time.
Let this be
the last time we wake, and still

the wrens would nest,
the lilacs climb, the moonflowers open
at evening.

That was why he came: to show
the children stumbling from their slumber,
the mourners kneeling by the gravesides,

the lovers reaching, alone, for the empty
sheets, that everything, everything
is no one's, that our one work,

wholly, is to open,
and that nothing in this thirst-world
isn't broken

or needs to come again to be divine.

VI

SEPTEMBER

And now the first winds
purr what they've been learning
like a children's choir
flipping through their hymnals.

This test again, this wintering,
this bite.

Summer, Summer's roads are over—

And all these leaves,
this foliage on your shoulders—
like all the ghosts of childhood's
wild silence
laying on their hands
as though to guide you.
It is time to fall into your life.

LINES FOR MY CHILD TO CARRY WHEN LEAVING HOME

Go, my only,
go.

Go learn in the darkness
what the heart is:

not a book,
not a door,
not a blossom—

but the only thing
in this ruinous
universe
that can open again
knowing
                why it closed.

TO THE LOVER WHO LEFT ME FLOWERS IN A PEPSI BOTTLE, APOLOGIZING FOR HAVING NO VASE

If this is the truth, I want it.

Listen: I have wasted
my little life—
on spectacle, on golden lies,
on dust.

I know now
what your hands knew
when you did this:

Love
is the daily
bread, the make-it-work.

Touch me till this world is world enough.

VULNERABILITY

I could tell you
there is water
that you carry.
I could show you
the barn door broken open.
I could say that there is wildfire
in my land.

But enough of that, enough
of that, that tell-it-slant.
My heart-barn's burning horses want your hands.
My heart-barn's burning horses want your hands.

SPRING

after Jung

You have come this far
through darkness.
Rest, now,
in the lemon-scent
of the river.
Lie down
with the briars in your hair.

Listen: the wind
on the far shore,
stunned as the first touch of a lover.

Wherever your fear is,
your terror,
your life has always been there.

THE PRODIGAL ONE

What no one knows is
I didn't leave for pleasure.
I left because one morning I was woken.
I left because I heard a voice
that frightened me.
I ran out, tattered, mad
to be the wind.

(You know as well as I do
what those years were:
empty beds, a broken mirror, whiskey).

You, too, can return now.
Stand there at the small gate
of the garden
and listen to the voices in the kitchen.
You still have your life,
you still do.
All those years you thought
that you had lost it,
all those years of darkness
it was with you.
It was with you—you hear me?—as the great fear.
Go back into that first house of shadows.
Even if it's only ghosts
in the old rooms,
go to them
and dance them with beginnings.
Be the one great song you've always been.

TO MY ILLNESS

I have gone with you
all the way
through the dark
just to get
to the hour
at the end
when I will
feel myself
slipping from
your grip,
just to learn
I was not the same as you.

LATE HYMN

Sooner or later you will have to do it.
Go in. Open
the heavy door of childhood

and listen
to the same wind in the linens; listen
as it brings you to the bed again,

as you lie down
in the ruins of the new moon,
the new moon

with its bitter taste
of ashes, the tattered moon
with its silks

that bid you stay.
This
is the same moon, the moon of youth,

like all the heavy halters of a breaker.
This is the place
where the fear came, where it broke your life

like common bread
in darkness,
where it opened you

to the new moon in its changes. This
is where you gave your life
away.

Give in. Be still
and give in. Unlasting,
at last, is what you have now.

—And when you lie down
in the ruins
of this new moon, when you rise up

and stand again
in tatters,
look back

at the old ghosts
in the coldness,
the darkened house

of shadows as you close it,
as you open
to the spring wind

in the grasses, the cold road
you will walk, now, to its ending—
through the new

moon, through its ruins, through its music,
and as far as its changes will take you
toward the great

and the changed place
of the saved ones
where to live this life and sing it are the same.

THE WAY

They set off, by morning, in the gray dawn,
carrying the only things they called their own:
basket, compass, child.

In the fourth day they came, at last,
to a river, carried her water
for the child in her.

On the sixth day they fell again
in the old snow, looked at each other
and smiled. The immensity,

the great joke of being.
On the seventh day she failed to rise
in the gray wind. He found them

a dark barn in the deep drifts
and carried her inside
among the ox-stench

and laid her in the old hay
in the slatted light.
The heaviness, the slight lie

of arrival. The dying light
like honey in the rafters;
the taste of it

like cinnamon
and silver; the heft of it, the breath
of it; the hush.

Why should we show you
what it did to them? The rest of it
was fever dreams, was weakening.

They were found
in the last dawn of the second
age, she with her arms around her child,

he with his arms around
their coldness.
There are moments

when the flesh
is all we have left
and moments

when the spirit's blaze
can change us
and the moments

when the shape of our unknowing
is the same as the shape
of someone's fire

and that burning is eternity enough.

AFTER

What does it matter if you have not visited your life
in so long?

Go to it now.

You have lain, too long, in a house of shadows.

You have touched your face,
in the cracked glass, like a stranger.

You have listened
to the dark wind
of this land.

Go, now.
It is not too late
to enter.

Listen, they are still here,
the wild things.

Admit, admit, admit them:

Through the moon, through the moon's
spruce, they have come to you:

the spring mares
in no one's care, no master,

to bury their breath
in your fingers.

Absence, absence
crafts us
like the tender heft of a saddle-maker's hands.

THE SOURCE

Spring again, and I have come to the end
        of the river, the place
where the deer lay down their bones, where fireweed

        bursts through the leather
of old Chevys

and wild boys lay their buck-slugs
in the seat-backs—

where handprints smudge the dust
of windscreens
where a life, fresh-breathed, was entered
                by another, just to be deep

in the thrill of it, just to be someone, just to be here.

*

Silence
in the deep weeds, and for weeks
I've thought of the Goshen woods,
        of the mosses just north of Goshen, New York,
where I lay out, at seventeen,
        seven empty bridles in my hands. The horses
        were a neighbor's, and I had no stake in it

except everything, except that I guessed, as a child
        would,
        that nothing in this life would ever
not matter, the sound of rain
        in maples
        like your mother's voice the last time
        you heard it, a burning

in your hands you have no words for, the river
            through the trees like seven feral things
                        breathing, waiting, daring you to try.

Those were the longest nights of my life, no one
            around but the sap whispering in the larch-fire, the pulse
            of rain in the leaves,
            the faintest echo of coyotes on the far side of the mountain.

                        I didn't know how to enter a thing
any more than I knew how to leave one, but the Neversink
                        was the swiftest
it had been—boat-rot, old chains
            in its embankments—and those horses

            stomped and snorted in the darkness on the far
            shore, and how are the dead
                        not like the living—
                        how will they ever bring back themselves?

*

            Often, when the moon
            makes its way through the spruces
in this place
                        like someone carrying the brass, dismantled bed
            of someone or other's child, the night-birds
trilling in the dogwoods as they do
after snow, the first stars darkening
the branches,

I'm
twenty-five again, curled in a snow-squall in the lean-to
                        on Hunter Mountain, praying to outlast the night.
            I'd only gone up to leave my wedding ring
            and my own bones
                        and a note to be unfolded by
                                    the snows alone—

cedar-rot, the scent
of my own salt in my canvas pants,

but even the wind
        has a say, even the wind rubbing its bridleless face
        against those dovetails,

and without wishing it
                I was a child again, searching for those horses
                        on the far side of the river. Time
        is what we do with one another

and I remember how they fled from me
                when I climbed the bank, how poor
        we are, how the body belongs to no one.
    I remember there are laws we live by, and we almost know them.
        I remember knowing I would come back with nothing
                but dust, nothing but morning in my hands.

*

Spring again, and

it's madness, this life. It's buck-slugs in the old Chevy
        of your own heart, and when I hike out
and take the train
into the city
                and climb the stairs to shoulder open
this rented door, I can—tell it—I can smell my own breath
                in my plague mask, deep
                as cedar, trembling
        as the laurels on the far side of the mountain,

and I'm thirty again,
        lying out under the cold stars
                        of the Telegraph Pass, Alaska,
                the cold stars that were not the bones

of any father   in any river,
and I knew
                    it was time.
That was the longest night of my life, that briar, that fire

dying down, the stars
            like the lost ash of travelers,

and when I looked down
            in those waters—moonlight, blue
spruce, pine-sap—it was the face
        of the stranger who had led me, and he was
                older, more father
                than son now; he was
        not lost in that savage place; he was
                        not afraid
        and I

            sat back and left my bread
for what had carried me

            and I let the fire die
            for the final stars,
            and I sipped from the dark source
            of the river,
            and I followed him down the far side of the mountain.

*

Spring again,
and there comes a time
when the rain ceases in the grille-work
of this city
        and children are bickering in the alleys
and a hunger creeps into your gut
        you cannot explain, a burning

in your hands you cannot have back,
            the morning like a mare's chin
on your shoulder.

Twenty-five years ago I used to walk out into the dark
            and lift a saddle from the others
and cinch the girth into Cinnamon
                and ride up into the mountains and build a fire
        by that bend in the Neversink River
where someone hung a steering wheel
                in the branches
            and the scent is old leather

            and velvet
                and everything you've never hoped to enter.
        It is still there.
            I lost her
on the far side of the river

            and I'm told they found them
down in the talus across the county line, galloped
        all night from the callings
                    of some mad-eyed child,
        their bodies twisted in the stone-dust
of the quarry, the cliff-face rising
        slate and ancient in the morning light
            behind them, their roan coats salted
with labor,
                the briar of the long climb
                    in their knees.

*

    Listen, the wind says. Listen.

There are shattered pints
                and plague masks
                in the alleys.

    And the far stars
are still there in the clearings.

    And the river runs
             through the green weeds of the valley.

And the wind makes
            an old song
                in the oak groves—high up

    in the laurels
    and the blackthorn—

    calling
            on its wild way
            to the river,

    through the moon and the spruces
                and the lupine

    and the empty, blindered bridles in the trees.

THE RUBBLE OF NOTHING

Finally, at the end of every wreckage, we stand here
in these doomed rooms in moonlight
and tell ourselves we've done what we have wanted.

We say grief
is the worn boats in the harbor,
waiting to carry us to another shore.

If the heart, the dark heart,
is the empty page, we say love is the sea itself
with its voices, troubling the margin

as it rises, turning us
like a story we can't fathom.
This is the way, we say, the only way.

And if one day
we should waken
in the wreckage,

if we should turn back to the dark heave
of the harbor
and see nothing but the sea wind, the winters,

what does it matter
if it can't last,
if the journey, the way here, lies in ruins,

if the old life lies in carnage on the dark shore?
The men among the lilies
were our fathers; the hymns

we didn't open were our children; our mothers
were the light we didn't learn.
Listen, the wind sings. Listen.

Then we remember
that the body sings, that the lonely
have always been lonely,

that the troubled world is the rubble
of nothing—and that the singing, the singing
in the rigging, that soft song

in the cargo of our own hearts
is the one hymn, the one hymn
of the living, that luminous music

of departure, which is all we may know of return.

FOR THE END, WHENEVER IT MAY COME

All my life I heard a music
that almost carried me.

My mother's love
like cold sap in my branches.
My father's hush
as wild as foals, and strong.

From these
I made a little life
to give to you.

These
and this same soft voice
that wakens me:

Don't be afraid, Joseph.
The singing has to end
to be a song.

Coda

ORPHEUS IN STARLIGHT

And so they handed him the dark harp
of his own heart. At first
he was startled. At first
he lifted it to his face

and smelled the deep green of the willow branch
on which it had hung, all night, in the garden.
This is who you are, they said.
How could you have forgotten?

But he knew one song in him had ended.
He knew there is the singing of a life
and the great, good song of its living,
and so he hung the harp over his shoulder

and turned down into the underworld,
calling a name that was everything,
calling her until the dark god stepped forward
and told him, in clear tones, what he'd done.

Is this your life? the god asked.
Yes, was the answer. *This is what I want.*
And so it was arranged. The god, robed
in shadows, brought her forth,

her face hidden in the tall fronds
of the underworld. Orpheus
was allowed one glimpse, that's all,
and in his heart he knew all things that would happen.

Turn, the god said. *This is how it begins.*
And so they went. Why should we tell of it
any more than has been told? He broke
the way a mortal does, any mortal,

and when he turned back
there was only the clear path with its dark leaves
and the scent of her like apple trees in autumn.
He was alone. That's all. Even he

would not have remembered
the dark harp on his shoulder, his own heart,
had it not slid down into his hands
when he knelt, had it not

suddenly strummed itself
of its own accord, raising a song from his youth, a song
of gardens and horses, a song
he once had sung to her, a song

that broke him a second time
with its sweetness. And so he laid his hands
over the strings, to quiet them. He only knew
what all mourners know:

he would be turned into a story
and he was no story at all;
he would be turned into a song
though his heart now was the silence in all things.

That was all. He rose
and turned himself up the dark path
toward the sunlight,
and when he reached it

he lay down on the warm earth
with the dark harp of his own heart beside him.
Let the wind play it, he thought now.
I am done with it. I am done with it forever.

And he was. For long, cold hours,
he was done with it. There was no music
in the night birds in the spruces, no song
in the mountains

all around him, the cold waves
of the harbor far below him.
Even his dreams
were without hope. Even his deepest dreams.

But somewhere, in the darkness, he was startled.
He had dreamed of her
and he looked up
at the far stars.

There were many of them, bright and clear
and shining, brilliant
as the first fires of childhood.
He smelled, again, the silk scent

of her mending, the rich oil
of her dark hair in its ribbons, her true voice
like linnets in his own hands.
He did not choose. He lifted the harp

as he had to do
and drew from it the darkest song of his being.
He played it
all night, all morning, never knowing

if it was death he asked
or the end of death, never knowing
if the great songs have an answer. He played it
with all of him, then he rested.

In his silence, he had hardly noticed
what had come to him.
He lay the harp on the dark earth
and looked at them.

Is this the cost, he asked, *of my singing?*
But the Furies only looked at him in pity.
No, they said, as they laid their hands
upon him. *This is the price*

for what you did not live.
Wait, he said, and lifted up
the dark harp.
Tell me, is there any chance

for mercy? I loved the earth, and I chose my song
above her. Give me
just one more hour. Give me
just one more chance at being.

They looked at each other in the shadows.
Their words between them
like cold leaves rustling.
Like all his mother's honey

in the cellar. Like all his father's bridles
in the wind.
When they turned to him, they took away
his small harp. They knew, in their own hearts,

what they'd do to him.
But they gave it back
and backed away
and knelt for him.

They let him lift
his own heart in the darkness.
He looked down, and they had cut the strings
forever. *No*, he thought, and clasped it

to his empty chest.
No, he said, and he touched it
to his lips.
Listen, he told himself. *Just listen.*

And then, through the darkness, he heard them.
Astonish us, Death's messengers
called out to him.
And he closed his eyes

and told himself, with no one,
that the silence of any end or wreckage
is the same as the great and ancient silence
that comes before beginning starts to sing.

ACKNOWLEDGMENTS

The author would like to extend his gratitude to the editors of the following publications, in which the following poems—sometimes in earlier versions—were printed:

The Academy of American Poets: "For a Student Who Used AI to Write a Paper," "The Moon," "Hymn";

The Adroit Journal: "The Lions of Orange County";

American Poetry Journal: "Boy Leading a Horse";

Apple Valley Review: "Work";

Cider Press Review: "Psalm," "After";

Columbia Journal: "Ovid Among the Birds of Tomis";

The Cortland Review: "Schumann to Clara—Bonn, 1856," "Desire: After Sappho";

East Ridge Review: "After Love," "Teaching My Son to Swim," "For the End, Whenever It May Come";

FemAsia: "After Love," "Words Whispered to a Child Under Siege," "The Last Love Poem";

Ice Floe: "Leda," "The Whale Skeleton on Long Branch Beach," "Genie Wiley";

Leavings: "Penelope," "Inventory," "Late Hymn," "The Garden," "Pietà," "Migrations";

The Meadow: "Lines Written in a Time of Pandemic," "Childhood," "The Source," "Narcissus," "The Vow";

Measure: "Sonnet to My Dead Interrupted by a Doe in Forsythia";

The Normal School: "Trying to Translate Yesenin's Death Poem";

Passages North: "Triumph";

RATTLE: "Hymn," "Saint Vitus' Dance," "Caril Anne Fugate," "What to Say to Those Who Think You're a Fool for Choosing Poetry";

The 'Read' Carpet, an International Journal: "Late Hymn," "Orpheus," "Coda";

The Scores: "The Middle of the Way," "Letter to Lorca Written on His Piano, Granada, 2019";

South Florida Poetry Journal: "Poppies," "The Moon";
Thrush: "Wheat Field with Crows," "At Wolf Lake";
VerseVille: "The Way."

"Holy Saturday" was printed in *Edebiyat Ortami* in a Turkish translation by Aycan Gürlüyer. "Wheat Field with Crows" and "Lines Written in a Time of Pandemic" were nominated for the Pushcart Prize. "Letter to Lorca Written on His Piano, Granada, 2019" was highly commended for the Forward Prize for Best Single Poem and was reprinted in *The Forward Book of Poetry 2022* (Faber and Faber). "For a Student Who Used AI to Write a Paper" appeared in a Spanish translation by Joan Pablo Carillo Hernandez in *PajamaSurf*. "The Source" is indebted to Charles Wright. "Triumph" quotes James Dickey's "Cherrylog Road" in line five. "After Sappho" is indebted to Richmond Lattimore's translation of "φαίνεταί μοι."

The author extends his gratitude to Laura Garcia Lorca, whose hospitality made "Letter to Lorca" possible; to the late Lucie Brock-Broido and Mark Strand, whose friendship and guidance remain; to Kevin McGrath, who was always there; and to all who helped in the production of this book, especially Peter Conners and the team at BOA Editions.

ABOUT THE AUTHOR

Joseph Fasano's previous books of poetry include *The Crossing* (2018), *Vincent* (2015), *Inheritance* (2014), and *Fugue for Other Hands* (2013). His novels include *The Swallows of Lunetto* (2022) and *The Dark Heart of Every Wild Thing* (2020). His honors include the Cider Press Review Book Award, the Rattle Poetry Prize, and a nomination by Linda Pastan for the Poets' Prize, "awarded annually for the best book of verse published by a living American poet two years prior to the award year." His writing has appeared in *The Yale Review, The Times Literary Supplement, The Missouri Review, Boston Review, American Literary Review, Tin House, The Adroit Journal, American Poets Magazine,* and many other publications. His prose and poetry have been widely translated and anthologized, most recently in *The Forward Book of Poetry* (Faber and Faber). He is also the author of *The Magic Words* (TarcherPerigee, 2024), a collection of poetry prompts and exercises that help people of all ages unlock their creativity.

BOA Editions, Ltd. American Poets Continuum Series

174

COLOPHON

BOA Editions, Ltd., a not-for-profit publisher of
poetry and other literary works, fosters readership and
appreciation of contemporary literature. By identifying,
cultivating, and publishing both new and established poets
and selecting authors of unique literary talent, BOA brings
high-quality literature to the public.

Support for this effort comes from the sale of its publications,
grant funding, and private donations.

*

*The publication of this book is made possible, in part,
by the special support of the following individuals:*

Anonymous
Blue Flower Arts, LLC
Angela Bonazinga & Catherine Lewis
Susan Burke, *in honor of Boo Poulin*
Mr. & Mrs. P. David Caccamise, *in memory of
Dr. Gary H. Conners*
Daniel R. Cawley
Bonnie Garner
Margaret B. Heminway
Charles Hertrick & Joan Gerrity
Grant Holcomb, *in memory of Robert & Willy Hursh*
Nora A. Jones
Paul LaFerriere & Dorrie Parini, *in honor of Bill Waddell*
Jack & Gail Langerak
Barbara Lovenheim
Joe McElveney
Daniel M. Meyers, in honor of J. Shepard Skiff
Boo Poulin
John H. Schultz
William Waddell & Linda Rubel
Michael Waters & Mihaela Moscaliuc